MONTHLY PLANNER 2015

Month of:______________________________

Sunday	Monday	Tuesday	Wednesday	Thursday	Friday	Saturday

Monthly Goals

Month of:________________________

Sunday	Monday	Tuesday	Wednesday	Thursday	Friday	Saturday

Monthly Goals

Month of:________________________

Sunday	Monday	Tuesday	Wednesday	Thursday	Friday	Saturday

Monthly Goals

Month of:______________________________

Sunday	Monday	Tuesday	Wednesday	Thursday	Friday	Saturday

Monthly Goals

Month of:______________________________

Sunday	Monday	Tuesday	Wednesday	Thursday	Friday	Saturday

Monthly Goals

____

____

____

____

____

____

____

____

____

____

____

____

____

Month of:______________________________

Sunday	Monday	Tuesday	Wednesday	Thursday	Friday	Saturday

Monthly Goals

Month of:____________________________

Sunday	Monday	Tuesday	Wednesday	Thursday	Friday	Saturday

Monthly Goals

Month of:________________________

Sunday	Monday	Tuesday	Wednesday	Thursday	Friday	Saturday

Monthly Goals

Month of:______________________________

Sunday	Monday	Tuesday	Wednesday	Thursday	Friday	Saturday

Monthly Goals

Month of:____________________________

Sunday	Monday	Tuesday	Wednesday	Thursday	Friday	Saturday

Monthly Goals

Month of:____________________

Sunday	Monday	Tuesday	Wednesday	Thursday	Friday	Saturday

Monthly Goals

Month of:______________________________

Sunday	Monday	Tuesday	Wednesday	Thursday	Friday	Saturday

Monthly Goals

Month of:____________________________

Sunday	Monday	Tuesday	Wednesday	Thursday	Friday	Saturday

Monthly Goals

Month of:______________________________

Sunday	Monday	Tuesday	Wednesday	Thursday	Friday	Saturday

Monthly Goals

Month of:____________________________

Sunday	Monday	Tuesday	Wednesday	Thursday	Friday	Saturday

Monthly Goals

Month of:________________________________

Sunday	Monday	Tuesday	Wednesday	Thursday	Friday	Saturday

Monthly Goals

____

____

____

____

____

____

____

____

____

____

____

____

____

Month of:____________________________

Sunday	Monday	Tuesday	Wednesday	Thursday	Friday	Saturday

Monthly Goals

Month of:_________________________

Sunday	Monday	Tuesday	Wednesday	Thursday	Friday	Saturday

Monthly Goals

Month of:__________________________

Sunday	Monday	Tuesday	Wednesday	Thursday	Friday	Saturday

Monthly Goals

Month of:______________________________

Sunday	Monday	Tuesday	Wednesday	Thursday	Friday	Saturday

Monthly Goals

____

____

____

____

____

____

____

____

____

____

____

____

____

Month of:____________________________

Sunday	Monday	Tuesday	Wednesday	Thursday	Friday	Saturday

Monthly Goals

Month of:____________________________

Sunday	Monday	Tuesday	Wednesday	Thursday	Friday	Saturday

Monthly Goals

Month of:______________________________

Sunday	Monday	Tuesday	Wednesday	Thursday	Friday	Saturday

Monthly Goals

____

____

____

____

____

____

____

____

____

____

____

____

____

Month of:____________________

Sunday	Monday	Tuesday	Wednesday	Thursday	Friday	Saturday

Monthly Goals

Month of: ______________________

Sunday	Monday	Tuesday	Wednesday	Thursday	Friday	Saturday

Monthly Goals

____

____

____

____

____

____

____

____

____

____

____

____

____

Month of:______________________________

Sunday	Monday	Tuesday	Wednesday	Thursday	Friday	Saturday

Monthly Goals

Month of:____________________________

Sunday	Monday	Tuesday	Wednesday	Thursday	Friday	Saturday

Monthly Goals

Month of:______________________________

Sunday	Monday	Tuesday	Wednesday	Thursday	Friday	Saturday

Monthly Goals

Month of:____________________

Sunday	Monday	Tuesday	Wednesday	Thursday	Friday	Saturday

Monthly Goals

Month of:______________________________

Sunday	Monday	Tuesday	Wednesday	Thursday	Friday	Saturday

Monthly Goals

Month of:______________________________

Sunday	Monday	Tuesday	Wednesday	Thursday	Friday	Saturday

Monthly Goals

Month of:______________________________

Sunday	Monday	Tuesday	Wednesday	Thursday	Friday	Saturday

Monthly Goals

Month of:______________________________

Sunday	Monday	Tuesday	Wednesday	Thursday	Friday	Saturday

Monthly Goals

____

____

____

____

____

____

____

____

____

____

____

____

____

Month of:______________________________

Sunday	Monday	Tuesday	Wednesday	Thursday	Friday	Saturday

Monthly Goals

Month of:______________________________

Sunday	Monday	Tuesday	Wednesday	Thursday	Friday	Saturday

Monthly Goals

____

____

____

____

____

____

____

____

____

____

____

____

____

Month of:______________________________

Sunday	Monday	Tuesday	Wednesday	Thursday	Friday	Saturday

Monthly Goals

Month of:________________________

Sunday	Monday	Tuesday	Wednesday	Thursday	Friday	Saturday

Monthly Goals

Month of:____________________________

Sunday	Monday	Tuesday	Wednesday	Thursday	Friday	Saturday

Monthly Goals

Month of:________________________

Sunday	Monday	Tuesday	Wednesday	Thursday	Friday	Saturday

Monthly Goals

Month of:________________________

Sunday	Monday	Tuesday	Wednesday	Thursday	Friday	Saturday

Monthly Goals

Month of:______________________________

Sunday	Monday	Tuesday	Wednesday	Thursday	Friday	Saturday

Monthly Goals

Month of:______________________________

Sunday	Monday	Tuesday	Wednesday	Thursday	Friday	Saturday

Monthly Goals

Month of:____________________

Sunday	Monday	Tuesday	Wednesday	Thursday	Friday	Saturday

Monthly Goals

Month of:____________________

Sunday	Monday	Tuesday	Wednesday	Thursday	Friday	Saturday

Monthly Goals

Month of:______________________________

Sunday	Monday	Tuesday	Wednesday	Thursday	Friday	Saturday

Monthly Goals

____

____

____

____

____

____

____

____

____

____

____

____

____

Month of:__________________________

Sunday	Monday	Tuesday	Wednesday	Thursday	Friday	Saturday

Monthly Goals

Month of:____________________

Sunday	Monday	Tuesday	Wednesday	Thursday	Friday	Saturday

Monthly Goals

Month of:____________________

Sunday	Monday	Tuesday	Wednesday	Thursday	Friday	Saturday

Monthly Goals

www.ingramcontent.com/pod-product-compliance
Lightning Source LLC
LaVergne TN
LVHW082301150826
845677LV00009B/1683

* 9 7 9 8 8 6 9 4 5 5 2 1 5 *